PU

Jeremy STRONG
LAUGH-YOUR-SOCKS-OFF
Even More
Joke Book

Jeremy Strong once worked in a bakery, putting the jam into three thousand doughnuts every night. Now he puts the jam in stories instead, which he finds much more exciting. At the age of three, he fell out of a first-floor bedroom window and landed on his head. His mother says that this damaged him for the rest of his life and refuses to take any responsibility. He loves writing stories because he says it is 'the only time you alone have complete control and can make anything happen'. His ambition is to make you laugh (or at least snuffle). Jeremy Strong lives near Bath with his wife, Gillie, four cats and a flying cow.

Are you feeling silly enough to read more?

THE BEAK SPEAKS
CHICKEN SCHOOL
DINOSAUR POX
GIANT JIM AND THE HURRICANE
I'M TELLING YOU, THEY'RE ALIENS!
THE INDOOR PIRATES
THE INDOOR PIRATES ON TREASURE ISLAND
KRANKENSTEIN'S CRAZY HOUSE OF HORROR
KRAZY KOW SAVES THE WORLD – WELL, ALMOST
LET'S DO THE PHARAOH!
PANDEMONIUM AT SCHOOL
PIRATE PANDEMONIUM
THE SHOCKING ADVENTURES OF LIGHTNING LUCY
THERE'S A PHARAOH IN OUR BATH!
THERE'S A VIKING IN MY BED AND OTHER STORIES
TROUBLE WITH ANIMALS

Read more about Streaker's adventures:
THE HUNDRED-MILE-AN-HOUR DOG
RETURN OF THE HUNDRED-MILE-AN-HOUR DOG
WANTED! THE HUNDRED-MILE-AN-HOUR DOG
LOST! THE HUNDRED-MILE-AN-HOUR DOG

Read more about Nicholas's daft family:
MY DAD'S GOT AN ALLIGATOR!
MY GRANNY'S GREAT ESCAPE
MY MUM'S GOING TO EXPLODE!
MY BROTHER'S FAMOUS BOTTOM
MY BROTHER'S FAMOUS BOTTOM GETS PINCHED!
MY BROTHER'S FAMOUS BOTTOM GOES CAMPING
MY BROTHER'S HOT CROSS BOTTOM

Jeremy STRONG'S

LAUGH-YOUR-SOCKS-OFF

Even More

Joke

Book

Pranks with and Bottoms!

PUFFIN

PUFFIN BOOKS

Published by the Penguin Group
Penguin Books Ltd, 80 Strand, London WC2R 0RL, England
Penguin Group (USA) Inc., 375 Hudson Street, New York, New York 10014, USA
Penguin Group (Canada), 90 Eglinton Avenue East, Suite 700, Toronto, Ontario,
Canada M4P 2Y3 (a division of Pearson Penguin Canada Inc.)
Penguin Ireland, 25 St Stephen's Green, Dublin 2, Ireland
(a division of Penguin Books Ltd)
Penguin Group (Australia), 250 Camberwell Road, Camberwell, Victoria 3124,
Australia (a division of Pearson Australia Group Pty Ltd)
Penguin Books India Pvt Ltd, 11 Community Centre, Panchsheel Park,
New Delhi – 110 017, India
Penguin Group (NZ), 67 Apollo Drive, Rosedale, North Shore 0632, New Zealand
(a division of Pearson New Zealand Ltd)
Penguin Books (South Africa) (Pty) Ltd, 24 Sturdee Avenue, Rosebank,
Johannesburg 2196, South Africa

Penguin Books Ltd, Registered Offices: 80 Strand, London WC2R 0RL, England

puffinbooks.com

First published 2009
003

Copyright © Puffin Books, 2009
Introduction and short story copyright © Jeremy Strong, 2009
Illustrations copyright © Nick Sharratt, Rowan Clifford, Ian Cunliffe, 2009
Based on Jeremy Strong's books, copyright © Jeremy Strong
Compiled and designed by Perfect Books Ltd
All rights reserved

The moral right of the author and illustrators has been asserted

Set in Sabon, Utopia, Ad Lib and Bokka
Made and printed in England by Clays Ltd, St Ives plc

British Library Cataloguing in Publication Data
A CIP catalogue record for this book is available from the British Library

ISBN: 978-0-141-32798-3

www.greenpenguin.co.uk

MIX
Paper from
responsible sources
FSC
www.fsc.org   FSC™ C018179

Penguin Books is committed to a sustainable
future for our business, our readers and our planet.
This book is made from Forest Stewardship
Council™ certified paper.

Contents

Contents

Introduction

Life is full of choices. Should I have cereal or toast for breakfast? Should we get an alligator as a pet, or a chimpanzee? Do I want to learn how to be a pirate at school, or shall I turn into a dinosaur and terrify the head teacher?

The way to decide between two choices, of course, is with one simple question: which is better?

That's what this book is all about. Which is better – Christmas or birthdays? Pharaohs or Vikings? Grannies or babies? It's up to you to decide, but to help there are book extracts, pranks to play, games and puzzles to work out and LOADS of jokes!

Perfect Pranking

Always think before you prank!

choose your target: someone that won't get too frightened or upset, and will see the funny side . . . eventually. So not Mr Tugg then.

choose your location: some pranks could get messy, so don't get into extra trouble by doing them on the new carpet.

choose your prank: don't try anything that could hurt someone else – or you.

choose your partner: pulling pranks with a mate can double the fun. But check with an adult if you're not sure about anything. Don't be surprised if Dad wants to help!

Take the consequences: you may end up being told off, or get targetted for more pranks. So make sure it's worth it!

Pirates vs Teachers

Ooh, this is tricky. Which is better, pirates or teachers? You can't beat a pirate for laughs.

How about Captain Blackpatch, the Indoor Pirate, who doesn't like water and only has baths with his clothes on? Or Patagonia Clatterbottom, the scary head of Pirate School, who rolls around in a boat-pram? Oh no – she's a teacher AND a pirate.

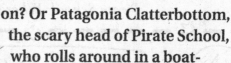

Then there's Violet Pandemonium, who gets her class to dress up as pirates and hide treasure in the school. Help, this is all mixed up!

Patagonia introduced her staff to the inspectors.

'Mrs Muggwump and her toucan teach rope-swinging, Mad Maggott does walking the gangplank and this is Miss Fishgripp. She teaches hand-to-hand fighting.'

Miss Piefinger sniffed loudly. 'And who teaches sailing?'

'I do,' said Patagonia, who was probably the world's worst sailor.

Pirate School: Where's That Dog?

Why is Patagonia's bum so big? **She's grabbed a lot of booty.**

I know a pirate with a wooden leg called Clatterbottom.

Really, what's her other leg called?

Where does Captain Blackpatch keep his treasure chest? **Inside his treasure shirt.**

How do you spot a short-sighted pirate?
He's got a bifocal eye patch.

Is it expensive to join a pirate ship?
Arr yes. It'll cost you an arm and a leg.

Captain, where do pirates go to exercise?

Our gym, lad!

This a very fuel-efficient pirate ship.
It does sixty miles to the galleon.

What do you call a pirate who is missing an eye?
Prate.

☆ 3 ☆

Do you think you could ever give up being a pirate?

No, I'm hooked.

Why did the pirate cross the ocean?
To get to the other tide.

What lies at the bottom of the ocean and shakes?
A nervous wreck.

What do you call a pirate with two eyes and two legs?
A trainee.

How do you know if you're a pirate?
If you AAAARGH, you are.

Inside Mrs Earwigger's classroom you could have heard a pin drop. Mrs Earwigger stared at the classroom door as if it had just stuck its tongue at her and burped, very loudly. The children stared at Mrs Earwigger, wondering what she would do next, glancing at each other, with tiny smiles hiding on their lips.

Then Mrs Earwigger's mouth began to do something very strange.

Pirate Pandemonium

How many head teachers does it take to change a light bulb? **Two: one to call the caretaker, and one to blame the pupils.**

Stop whistling while you're working, Tim!

Oh, it's OK, sir. I wasn't working.

My teacher's rubbish. She doesn't know anything — she keeps asking us questions.

I thought I told you to go and stand at the back of the line!

I tried to, sir, but there was already someone there.

My teacher really likes me. She keeps putting kisses on my homework.

This homework looks like your mum's handwriting.

Of course it does — I borrowed her pen.

I'd like you to tell me what 'coincidence' means.

How strange, I was just going to ask you the same thing.

How many letters are there in the alphabet?
Eleven. T, H, E, A, L, P, H, A, B, E and T.

Did you hear about the cross-eyed teacher?
She couldn't control her pupils.

What's two plus two?

Four.

Yes, that's good.
Good? It's perfect!

Rob! I hope I didn't just see you looking at Sophie's answers.

I hope you didn't see me either, miss.

If you add 34.75 and 4,097, then divide by 4, what would you get?

The wrong answer.

Questions Teachers Hope Pupils Won't Ask

Why doesn't glue stick to the inside of the bottle?

If clouds and rain are both water, why do clouds stay up in the air and rain falls to the ground?

If the corner shop is open twenty-four hours a day, every day of the year, why does it have locks on the doors?

What sticks the non-stick coating on to non-stick pans?

If you are in a car travelling at the speed of light, what happens if you turn on the headlights?

What do farmers plant when they want to grow seedless grapes?

Why do they put lifejackets under the seats in planes, not parachutes?

Would the ocean be deeper if it didn't have sponges in it?

Tricky Treasure

First, the secret preparation. Get a ten pence coin and a pencil. Rub the pencil around the rim of the coin, getting as much graphite on the edge as possible.

Challenge your sister. Hold another ten pence coin between your thumb and finger, and roll it down your forehead and nose, over your mouth and down to the chin. Bet that they can't do the same thing without letting go or missing a bit.

Give them the marked coin. With luck, they'll leave a thin black line down the middle of their face.

Odd-Pirate-Out

Here are the Indoor Pirates. Can you find one
picture in each set that is different from the rest?

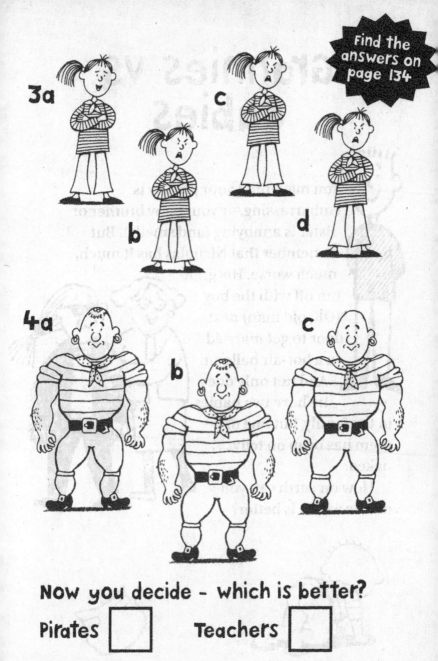

Find the answers on page 134

3a   c

b   d

4a   b   c

Now you decide – which is better?

Pirates ☐   Teachers ☐

Grannies VS Babies

You may think your granny is embarrassing, or your baby brother or sister is annoying (and smelly). But remember that Nicholas has it much, much worse. His gran ran off with the boy (OK, old man) next door to get married in a hot-air balloon. And not only does he have two babies in the family, but one of them has been on telly . . . naked.

How on earth can you decide which is better?

Do you know what she did next? She whispered into my left ear, 'Do you think he fancies me, Nicholas?'

I tried to escape, but she clung on to me. 'You've gone very red, Nicholas. You're not embarrassed by your granny, are you?' Embarrassed? I wanted to crawl into a hole and hide. Come to think of it I wanted my granny to crawl into a hole and hide.

My Granny's Great Escape

How old's your granny?

I don't know, but when we lit all the candles on her birthday cake her wig melted.

Ooh, we're going too fast! We're going to crash! Oh, I can't watch!

Look, perhaps I'd better drive then.

My gran's got a very thin body and a big round head. **She's a lollipop lady.**

How many grans does it take to change a light bulb?
Two: one to change the bulb, one to go on about how much better bulbs were in the old days.

Do you know the three signs that you're getting old?

No, what are they?

Well, there's memory loss. And, er ... I forget the other one.

Ooh, isn't it windy?

No, it's Thursday.

So am I – let's have a cup of tea.

Do you know how we knew Gran had a boyfriend?
Two sets of teeth in the glass by her bed.

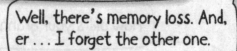
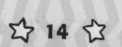

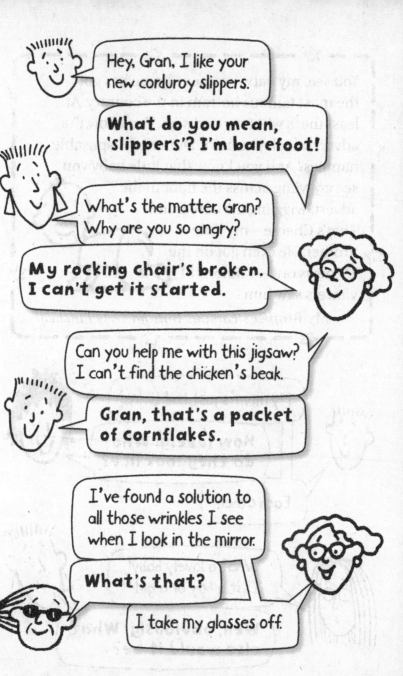

You see, my baby brother Cheese has got the most famous bottom in the country. At least that's what my dad says. You know that advert on television for Dumpers disposable nappies? And you know that little baby you see crawling across the floor in the advert, wiggling his bare bum? That's Cheese – my little brother! He even got on the TV news once. Millions of viewers saw him.

My Brother's Famous Bottom Gets Pinched!

My mum's just had twins!

How lovely. Who do they look like?

Each other.

What a lovely baby! Is it a boy or a girl?

Well, obviously. What else would it be?

How many babysitters does it take to change a light bulb? **None, they can't get the nappy to stay on.**

What musical instrument is Cheese learning? **The trump-et.**

What colour are Tomato's burps? **Burple.**

How good are Cheese and Tomato at football? **Well, they can dribble.**

What did Cheese call Tomato when she fell in a cowpat? **'You incowpoop.'**

My parents are about to start potty training. It's about time too. I mean, they're going to have to teach the twins soon.

We've been short of money since the twins were born. They've had to share a nappy – it's the only way we could make ends meet.

When one of the babies cries in the night, who gets up? **All of us.**

Knock-knock!

Who's there?

I done up.

I done up who?

I wondered what the smell was.

Toilet Trail

Cheese wants to start toilet training. Which trail should he follow if he wants to get to the loo?

POO!

Spot the Difference

Aah, how lovely. Gran and Lancelot have finally got married! Can you spot six differences between these two pictures?

Now you decide - which is better?

Grannies ☐   Babies ☐

School vs Hospital

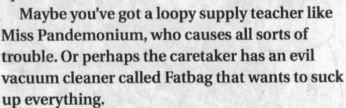

Which one is better: school or hospital? Neither sounds much fun at all, to be honest – but it depends what you get up to.

Maybe you've got a loopy supply teacher like Miss Pandemonium, who causes all sorts of trouble. Or perhaps the caretaker has an evil vacuum cleaner called Fatbag that wants to suck up everything.

On the other hand, if you're stuck in hospital for five weeks, perhaps you've got a silent friend from Mars to keep things interesting. Or you've rushed to hospital behind a pizza delivery van because your mum's giving birth to twins!

The ambulance growled, scrunged its gears, leaped down the school drive and skidded to a halt in the car park.

A short figure jumped out, pulling six assorted bags after her and spilling half of them on to the tarmac. She gazed around for a moment and ran a hand through a head of hair that looked like a rook's nest. She had lipstick halfway up one cheek and eyeshadow over most of her nose. She gave Mr Shrapnell a cheery grin and staggered across the playground towards him, trailing bags behind.

'Morning!' she cried. 'What a lovely morning too – Violet Pandemonium – how do you do?'

Pandemonium at School

Why did the jelly baby go to school?
Because he wanted to be a Smartie.

Where does a school keep all the books that aren't true?
In the lie-brary.

What did you learn at school today?

Not enough, it seems. I've got to go back tomorrow.

Why are you late every day?

Because the sign outside school says 'Go Slow, Children'.

I can't go to school today. I don't feel well.

Where don't you feel well?

In school.

What's the difference between a school bus driver and a cold? **One of them knows the stops and the other one stops the nose.**

So, do you like going to school?

 Going to school is fine, and coming home is even better. It's just the bit in between I don't like.

How come you've come home all cut and bruised?

 We had a class trip.

 That school uniform cost a fortune. Don't come home with a hole in the knee.

OK. Where would you like the hole then?

Dad says he's plain fed up.

'I'm fed up with you ending up in hospital,' he says. (See, told you.) 'I spend more time here than I do at home, all because of you.'

'Dad, you're exaggerating.'

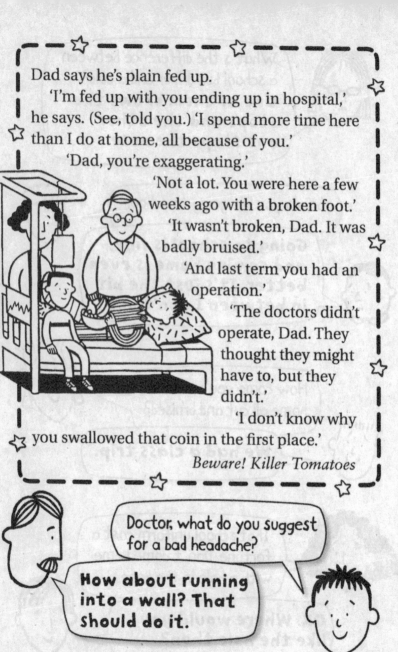

'Not a lot. You were here a few weeks ago with a broken foot.'

'It wasn't broken, Dad. It was badly bruised.'

'And last term you had an operation.'

'The doctors didn't operate, Dad. They thought they might have to, but they didn't.'

'I don't know why you swallowed that coin in the first place.'

Beware! Killer Tomatoes

Doctor, what do you suggest for a bad headache?

How about running into a wall? That should do it.

Nurse, whenever I drink tea I get a stabbing pain in my eye.

Have you tried taking the spoon out?

Doctor, I keep forgetting things.

I see. When did this start happening?

When did what start happening?

Nurse, I've got a carrot up my nose, a banana in one ear and a sausage in the other.

Your problem is that you're not eating properly.

☆ 27 ☆

Doctor, everyone keeps ignoring me.

Next!

Nurse, everyone says I'm bonkers because I like sausages.

There's nothing wrong with that. I like sausages too.

Really? Come and see my collection – I've got thousands!

Doctor, I think I'm losing my memory.

You certainly are – you told me that four jokes ago.

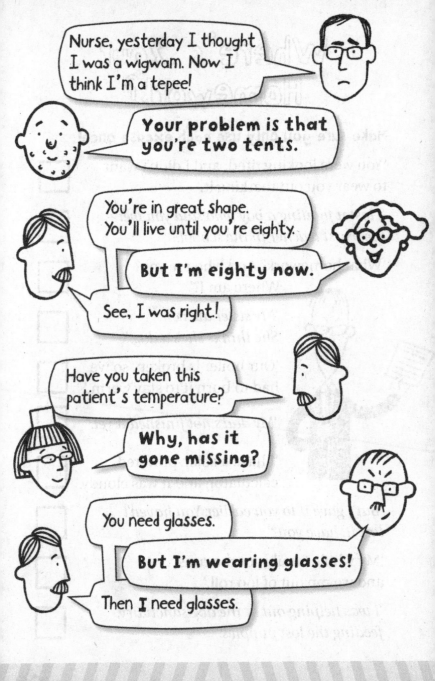

Where's Your Homework?

Make sure you only use each excuse once!

'You were looking tired, and I didn't want to wear you out marking it.'

'I lost it fighting a boy who said you were the worst teacher in the school.'

'What homework? And who are you? Where am I?'

'My sister ate it. She thinks she's a dog.'

'Our boiler is broken, so we had to burn it to stay warm.'

'My dad's not finished it yet.'

'I have a solar-powered calculator, and it was cloudy.'

'But I gave it to you earlier. You haven't lost it, have you?'

'My whole family got the runs and we ran out of loo roll.'

'I was helping out at the dog sanctuary, feeding the lost puppies.'

Bottle Rocket

This is more of a science trick than a prank, but it's still pretty funny. You need an adult to help, some vinegar, and some bicarbonate of soda (it's a white powder used for cooking – look in the cupboard).

Find a small plastic bottle and half fill it with vinegar. You need to tip a big spoonful of bicarbonate into the bottle quickly – it'll be easier if you can find a small funnel, or roll some paper into a cone.

Stand back and see what happens. You can probably think of ways to improve on the effect. If you've seen a toy volcano kit, this is what makes the 'explosion'.

Don't forget to clean up, or you'll get into DEEP trouble!

School Search

Can you find these schoolish things in
the wordsearch below?
They may go up, down,
diagonally or backwards.

ASSEMBLY   BOOK
CLASS   DESK
HOMEWORK   LATE
LESSON   LUNCH   PLAYGROUND
PUPIL   TEACHER   UNIFORM

D	N	U	O	R	G	Y	A	L	P
A	M	R	O	F	I	N	U	T	A
T	E	A	C	H	E	R	K	S	S
P	Y	C	L	N	G	R	S	L	O
S	L	O	C	K	O	E	E	U	B
S	E	R	E	W	M	E	D	N	P
A	S	T	E	B	T	R	B	C	U
L	S	M	L	O	E	U	R	H	P
C	O	Y	A	O	T	Y	S	H	I
H	N	B	O	K	L	A	T	E	L

Bag the Booty

You're helping to load the car for a trip, carrying cases and bags. Bring out a completely empty suitcase, but pretend to struggle, as if it's so heavy you can hardly lift it (practise with a real heavy bag so you know how to act). Drop it down, saying you can't manage to carry the case any further.

Your big macho victim will call you a weed, go to jerk up the 'heavy' case and completely misjudge it.

They may even fall over, if you're lucky.

Now you decide – which is better?

School ☐   Hospital ☐

The Strange History of the cosmic Pyjamas

Part One

DATE: Five hundred million years ago. (In other words a very long time ago.)

Out in the far reaches of space a comet was streaking through the sky. It was huge. It was vast. And it was called Stanley. Nobody knew it was called Stanley because there were no people around at that time. Even the comet didn't know it was called Stanley because comets don't have brains. They can't *know* anything. So who called it Stanley? I did. I just felt it had to have a name. It makes things easier.

So, Stanley the comet was streaking through the sky. He looked pretty spectacular, with his long glittering trail of ice dust spread behind him. What a glorious sight. And then what happened? You won't believe this. There was another comet. There was! Two comets at the same time!

DATE: It's still a very, very long time ago, before humans.

Now, the other comet was called Henry. (Yes, I know, it's getting a bit like a Thomas the Tank Engine story, isn't it? But don't forget, these are comets we are talking about, not steam trains.) Anyhow, Henry

was even bigger than Stanley and they were set to pass very close to each other. They might even hit each other. Nobody knew what would happen because, like I said earlier, there weren't any people around to know.

In fact, they *didn't* hit each other, but Henry passed so close that the near miss changed Stanley's direction. Stanley altered course and set off in a slightly different direction. You might be thinking, *So what?* I will tell you.

DATE: Listen, it's STILL A VERY LONG TIME AGO - OK?

The new direction didn't matter for millions of miles. Stanley went on streaking through the silence of space for years and years without any trouble at all. But then something came in his way. It was something a great deal bigger than him. In fact, there was an entire planet in his way. And that planet was Earth.

Ah! There, you see? That's what happens sometimes. A tiny change of direction and years later – wallop! Stanley the comet crashes into Planet Earth. Well, it caused a bit of a commotion, I can tell you. The whole planet shook from top to bottom and back to the top again. Mountains cracked. Volcanoes blew up all over the place. Earthquakes shuddered here and there. Oceans disappeared and reappeared somewhere else.

As for poor old Stanley he was no more. He was a shattered comet and he lay there on the surface of the Earth in a billion trillion squillion crushed little bits of rock and ice that had come from the furthest reaches of the galaxy, and which were now scattered far and wide.

DATE: OK, it's only a million or so years ago now, probably about 11 March.

After that not a lot happened really. The dinosaurs came and went. Human beings arrived and began to mess things up the way they do, what with their little wars and big wars and so on.

It was when the humans began to try to grow things and make things that they made an odd discovery. Actually it was a very useful discovery. They found that in certain places you could grow things a lot more easily and the plants would be bigger than normal. And they also found that in certain places you could use rocks to make things – metal things.

In particular, the humans noticed that when they grew things where Stanley lay in about a billion bits and pieces, the plants did very well indeed. And when they used the bigger bits of rock left over from Stanley's little accident they made a rather special kind of metal called stannidium. They liked stannidium because it had a kind of strange glow to it.

Well, not a lot happened for a while. The people who liked growing things grew very big tomatoes and cabbages on the special bits of ground. And the people who liked making things used stannidium to make little models of the Eiffel Tower and the Statue of Liberty even though they hadn't yet been built. (Look, don't ask me how they knew about the Eiffel Tower and the Statue of Liberty if they hadn't been built. They just did, OK?)

DATE: The year 1305 - only 700 years ago. (That's almost yesterday!)

There was a farmer called Omar. He lived in Turkey. He had two wives, fifteen children, seventy-three goats and a rabbit called Stanley. (This is just coincidence. Stanley is a very common name for pet rabbits.) Anyhow, we're not bothered about his family and animals. Omar grew cotton and he grew his cotton on the earth made from Stanley. (That's Stanley the comet, not Stanley the rabbit. Do try to keep up.)

The cotton that Omar grew was used to make clothes. In fact, the cotton that Omar grew was very fine cotton and it was much in demand for making clothes. Most cotton in those days was used for making things like tea towels and tents and so on. Only the best cotton was used for clothes and Omar's cotton was the very, very best.

Meanwhile, in another part of Turkey (if you really must know, it was the bit over there), there was an old man called Ali. Now, Ali was an alchemist. Don't worry, I'll spell it for you – a-l-c-h-e-m-i-s-t. See? An alchemist is a kind of magician. They take all sorts of metals, plants and things that have come out of the ground and they try to make them into other things. What they would most like to make is gold. Alchemists are always trying to make gold. That's because they always need money because they have big houses and mortgages. (If you don't know what a mortgage is ask your parents.)

Anyhow, Ali was trying to make gold. He had ground down some stannidium until it was a fine glowing dust. He had mixed it with water and it made a dark liquid that only glowed every now and then. He was busily stirring a great tub of this mixture when the sleeve of his very fine robe dipped into the pot and soaked up some of the liquid. Now, it just so happened that Ali's robe was made from Omar's cotton.

Yes! You've worked it out, haven't you? You know what happened, don't you? What do you mean, you don't? YOU DON'T?! You haven't worked it out? All right, I will have to tell you.

When the cotton and the stannidium were put together something extraordinary happened. It was as if all the secrets of Space and Time – everything that Stanley (the comet, not the rabbit) had seen while travelling for those billions of years – had been locked away in the rock that Stanley once was. And now, when that very same rock was ground up and had been used to grow Omar's cotton, a kind of magic was released.

Ali looked at the dark stain on his robe. He looked again. It seemed to move. It seemed to quiver. And then it glowed. He touched it.

KERRANGGG BAM BOOLLIE BANG!

In an instant Ali was no longer in his big house. Instead he was flying through space. And he didn't have a spacesuit! Strange to tell, he didn't *need* a spacesuit. There he was, Ali the alchemist, drifting in outer space, among the stars. The things he saw! Amazing. The things he didn't see! (Rice pudding, elephants on pogo sticks and the invisible man, if you must ask.)

However, Ali got a bit tired of all this after a while. He was hungry too, and he began to wonder how he was going to get back to his big house to pay the mortgage. How was he supposed to get back? He couldn't see a single bus stop. The odd comet, including, funnily enough, Henry, went whizzing past but none of them were taking any passengers.

Ali looked at the sleeve of his robe that had caused all this trouble. The dark stain was glowing again. And then something else appeared on the sleeve. It was like the dark stain but it had a shape. It looked like a house. Ali's house. Two words appeared as well, winding their way slowly round the wedge of the glowing house. They said: *Touch me.*

So Ali did and:

GNAB EILLOOB MAB GGGNARREK!

(Kerranggg bam boollie bang, backwards.)

Ali was back in his house, hunched over his pot of liquid stannidium. Phew!

Well, as you can imagine, Ali had to go and have a lie down after all that. He also had a long think. And what Ali thought led to the strangest pair of pyjamas you could ever wish to see.

Find out more in Part Two of 'The Strange History of the Cosmic Pyjamas' on page 100!

DOGS VS BIRDS

Which is better, dogs or birds? It depends who you ask.

Trevor 'Two-Legs' Larkey loves his dog, Streaker, even though she's more trouble than a Mini full of monkeys. She's mostly greyhound, with a bit of Ferrari and quite a lot of whirlwind.

Dinah would say that birds are much better, but then she is a talking mynah bird. Captain Birdseye and Chicken Nugget, the chickens that Nicholas's dad got to make some money, turned out to be pretty stupid. But at least they did better than the poor birds in *Chicken School* (you'll have to read it to find out).

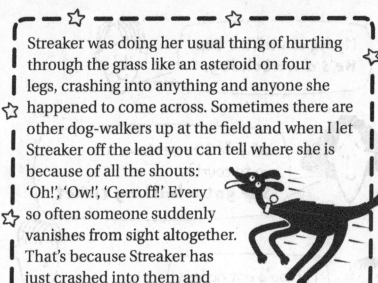

Streaker was doing her usual thing of hurtling through the grass like an asteroid on four legs, crashing into anything and anyone she happened to come across. Sometimes there are other dog-walkers up at the field and when I let Streaker off the lead you can tell where she is because of all the shouts: 'Oh!', 'Ow!', 'Gerroff!' Every so often someone suddenly vanishes from sight altogether. That's because Streaker has just crashed into them and knocked them flying.

Return of the Hundred-Mile-An-Hour Dog

What's brown and sticky?
A stick.

What's sticky and brown?
A sticky stick.

Why did Streaker say 'Meow'?
She was learning a foreign language.

My dog can tell the time. **He's a watchdog.**

 Why did Streaker have to go to court? **She got a barking ticket.**

My dog's got no legs.

Where did you find him?

Right where I left him.

How can I stop Streaker digging up the garden? **Take her spade away.**

What is Streaker's favourite pizza? **Pupperoni.**

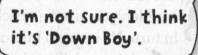
What's your name?

I'm not sure. I think it's 'Down Boy'.

Why did the dachshund bite his owner's ankle? **He couldn't reach any higher.**

Why does Streaker run in circles? **Well, have you tried running in squares?**

Why can't Dalmatians play Hide and Seek? **They're always spotted.**

The head teacher eyeballed Gary for several seconds and then his stare suddenly focused on each of us in turn. He lowered his voice to a sinister growl. 'So, what do you know about chickens, eh? Is there something funny about chickens and this school? Have any of you *seen* a chicken, maybe?'

Chicken School

What happens when a duck flies upside down?
It quacks up.

What did the chick say to the bully?
Peck on someone your own size.

A duck walked into a shop and asked for a lipstick.
'Certainly,' said the assistant.
'Will you be paying cash?'
'No, just put it on my bill.'

Why are birds so great?
Because they always suck seed.

How did the chicken feel after laying a hundred eggs?
Eggs-hausted.

Which seabird is short of breath?
A puffin.

What do you get if you cross a pigeon with a frog?
A pigeon-toed pigeon toad.

What is a polygon?
A dead parrot.

What do you get if you cross a parrot with a centipede?
A walkie-talkie.

Why do hummingbirds hum?
They can't remember the words.

What do you call a woodpecker with no beak?
A headbanger.

When's the best time to buy a budgie?
When they're going cheep.

Where do tough chickens come from?
Hard-boiled eggs.

Severed Finger

Cut a long oval hole in the bottom of an empty matchbox, and a round hole in the tray, so that you can tuck your middle finger into the box and open and close it. (Check with an adult before using scissors – they may want to help.) Tuck a bit of cotton wool round the finger to hide the hole. Dab on a bit of talc to make the finger pale, and add a bit of ketchup at the 'base' of your finger.

Run up to a friend and complain that a wild dog bit your finger off. Luckily you saved it – want to see? Open the matchbox. If he leans in close, wiggle the finger.

Animal Antics

Nicholas has quite a farm in his back garden.
There's a guard tortoise called Schumacher, a
goat, a cockerel and some chickens. Can you find
their names in the wordsnake opposite? Using
a pencil (in case you make a mistake) trace the
words, which are in the order shown below. The
words form a continuous line, snaking up and
down, back and forth, but never diagonally.
The line's been started for you!

**RUBBISH
CAPTAIN BIRDSEYE
POOP
MAVIS MOPPET
BEAKY
LEAKY**

R	U	A	P	Y	K
B	B	C	T	E	A
I	S	H	A	L	Y
I	B	N	I	A	K
R	E	Y	SECURITY	E	B
D	S	E	P	E	T
O	O	P	P	O	M
P	M	A	V	I	S

Paper Rain

PRANK!

You need lots and lots of tiny pieces of paper. If you can get hold of a hole punch, open it up to collect all the little circles of waste paper, or maybe you can find some confetti left over from a wedding. Otherwise just tear up some scrap paper.

Unroll a metre or so of loo roll on a table, and lay your paper bits on the flat bit (not too near the free end). Then roll the loo roll up neatly . . . and hang it back on the holder.

Someone's going to make a lovely mess pretty soon.

PRANK!

Paper Rain 2

If you've got some paper bits left over, the other great place to hide some is in an umbrella. Especially one of those little folding ones that your mum keeps in her handbag. You may have to imagine your mum's face when she sprinkles paper over her head at the first sign of rain.

Now you decide – which is better?

DOGS ☐   Birds ☐

Aliens vs Dinosaurs

Who would you prefer as a neighbour: aliens or dinosaurs?

Rob is pretty scared of aliens. Specifically, he's scared of the aliens that have moved in over the road. Especially after seeing a flying saucer hovering over their house. He's worried the Vorks are going to take over the world.

Mark, on the other hand, is pretty impressed when his sister Jodie turns into a dinosaur. He thinks it's the best thing she's ever done. And she begins to be nice to him, for a change.

There was something else nagging me too. If they were aliens, then what were they really like? Obviously their human form was just a disguise. What did they look like when they were not playing at being human? And why were they in such as rush to get home? I gazed out of the window, across the road, towards their house. I could see the slowly setting sun reflected in their windows.

And then all at once it came to me. Dracula! They were like vampires.

I'm Telling You, They're ALIENS!

What should you do if you see a spaceman? **Park in it, man.**

Why do aliens keep spilling their tea? **Because they've got flying saucers.**

If a meteorite misses the earth, is it a meteorong?

What do aliens do after they get married?
They go on their honeyearth.

What do little aliens get for doing their homework?
Gold stars.

Have you heard about the fantastic spaceship?
It was out of this world.

Where do aliens keep their sandwiches?
In a launchbox.

How do you get a baby alien to sleep?
Rock-et.

What's E.T. short for?
Because he's got little legs.

Oh no, a flying saucer has landed in the back garden!

You must have left the landing light on.

What did the alien say to the petrol pump?
Take your finger out of your ear and take me to your leader.

Mr Pinkerton-Snark poked and prodded Jodie all over until she began to feel like a pincushion, while Mr Bolton watched and waited nervously. He kept asking what was wrong with his daughter, and at length Mr Pinkerton-Snark announced his findings.

'She's a dinosaur,' he said.

'I would never have guessed,' Jodie grumbled darkly.

'We know that, but *why* is she a dinosaur?' said Mr Bolton.

'Huh!' squeaked the specialist. 'Why do children do anything?'

Dinosaur Pox

What do you get if you cross a Tyrannosaurus rex?
Eaten.

What does a triceratops sit on?
Its tricerabottom.

Why don't dinosaurs
eat clowns?
**Because they
taste funny.**

Why do they have old
dinosaur bones in the museum?
**They can't afford
new ones.**

What makes more noise
than a dinosaur?
Two dinosaurs.

Why did the dinosaur
sleep alone?
**He was a
brontosnore-us.**

Why do dinosaurs wear sandals?
So they don't sink in the sand.

Why do ostriches stick their heads in the sand?
They're looking for dinosaurs who forgot their sandals.

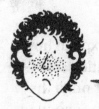

Do you know how long dinosaurs should be fed?
Exactly the same as short dinosaurs.

What did the dinosaur call her T-shirt shop?
'Try Sara's Tops'.

Alien Powers 1

Hold a broom in your left hand, standing with your left side to the audience. Hold your left wrist with your right hand, thumb on top. Your right forefinger should be hidden from the audience, so you can point it along your left wrist to hold the broom against your left hand.

Concentrate hard, and lift the broom off the ground. Then spread your left fingers out wide – the broom is 'stuck' to your hand. Make it look as if it's really hard to do.

Alien Powers 2

First rub your nose with your sleeve (to make sure it's not greasy). Then explain how meeting aliens has made you magnetic. Hold your head up straight, breathe gently on to the bowl of a clean teaspoon and hang the spoon on the end of your nose.

It works best if you've got a blobby kind of nose.

Alien Anagrams

The names of these planets have been mixed up.
Can you unscramble them?

THREA

TULPO

SRMA

SNEVU

CREMYUR

PEENNUT

STARUN

Monster Lunch

You may not be able to go to school as a dinosaur, but you can still freak your friends out with some disgusting things in your packed lunch. Persuade an adult to help with this lot.

Eyeballs

Use an apple corer to scoop a hole in a peeled lychee and pop in a bit of cherry (for the dark iris). Take a few in a plastic box containing a little raspberry juice.

Maggots

Cut up some cold cooked spaghetti into short pieces. Mix with Parmesan cheese and breadcrumbs. Eat with your fingers.

Dead man's fingers

Spread pâté on half of a slice of ham and add a thick line of squirty ketchup. Roll it up and stick a sliced almond on the end, as a fingernail.

Mouldy Sarnies

Use a cocktail stick to add drops of green food colouring to your bread, and the cheese inside the sandwich.

Dinomaze

Can you help Jodie get home to her family without getting caught by Mr Pinkerton-Snark?

Now you decide - which is better?

Aliens ☐   Dinosaurs ☐

Pharaohs VS Vikings

Who would you rather have come to live with you – a Viking or a pharaoh?

Sennapod (He Whose Name Shall Rumble Down The Ages) is a 4,600-year-old pharaoh from Ancient Egypt, protected by the Curse of Anubis. He's bossy and grumpy – but he loves computer games. Carrie and Ben get quite fond of him, really.

Sigurd (Siggy to his mates) is a proper Viking from a village in Denmark . . . a thousand years ago. No one's quite sure how he got here, but Tim and Zoe Ellis have a bundle of fun when he comes to live with them in the Viking Hotel.

The Pharaoh sat bolt upright, his haunting eyes fixing on all four of them at once with a commanding glare. Ben was almost certain he could see little red dots shooting out of Sennapod's eyes, which seemed to burn into his body, but it might just have been his imagination. The Pharaoh lifted a bony, half-bandaged arm and pointed at the Lightspeed family.

'Worms!' he roared, by way of saying hello. 'Do you dare raise your voices in front of the Pharaoh! Do you dare wage your puny wars before *me*!'

There's a Pharaoh in Our Bath!

Why was Professor Jelly, the archaeologist, so miserable?
His job was in ruins.

Sennapod loves chewy sweets shaped like babies' dummies.
He's a yummy gummy dummy mummy.

Why is Sennapod so tense?
He gets all wound up.

What colour is Sennapod's
cat when he's happy?
Purrrple.

Do mummies like being mummies?
Of corpse they do.

How does Sennapod get
milk from a cat?
He steals its saucer.

Apparently the undertakers buried
Sennapod in the wrong place.
**They were sacked for
making a grave mistake.**

Sennapod's cat ate the whole roast duck we got for lunch! **Now he's a duck-filled fatty-puss.**

What did the big pyramid say to the little pyramid? **'Where's your mummy?'**

What are Sennapod's favourite flowers? **Chrysanthemummies.**

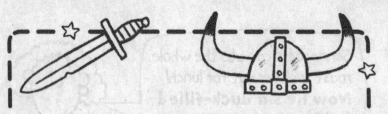

People came from far and wide to see Sigurd. He was, after all, quite a sight. He had a fearsome black beard and moustache and somehow managed to draw attention to himself wherever he went. This may have had something to do with the way he waved his huge sword 'Nosepicker' about his head.

Viking in Trouble

Siggy looks very impressive on a bicycle. **He's a striking biking Viking.**

What else does Siggy like to ride? **A Norse.**

Where do baby Vikings sleep? **In the Norsery.**

What do you call a Viking's wife?
A Viqueen.

How many Vikings does it take to change a light bulb?
None, they hadn't been invented.

Why did Siggy throw a loo roll down a hill?
He wanted it at the bottom.

Why hasn't Siggy tried waterskiing?
He couldn't find any sloping water.

Siggy walked into an antique shop.
'So what else is new?' he said.

Siggy, can you tell me if if my car indicators are working?

Yes ... no ... yes ... no ... yes ... no ... yes ... no ...

Which hand does Siggy use to stir his tea with? **Neither, he uses a spoon.**

What does Siggy do when it rains? **He gets wet.**

Why did Siggy buy a seahorse? **He wanted to play water polo.**

Half-made bed

Take the duvet off your visitor's bed. Untuck the bottom (foot end) of the sheet, fold it almost halfway up the bed and then tuck it back under the mattress at the sides. Put the duvet back over the half-sheet, making sure it hides the mattress at the bottom.

This works even better if the bed has blankets and a top sheet. Take off the blankets, hide the top sheet, fold up the bottom sheet so it looks like the top sheet and remake the bed.

PRANK!

Wake-up call

If your visitor has to get up early and needs an alarm clock, why not give him a little extra help? Get all the other alarms you can find in the house (don't forget the one on his mobile), and set them to go off five minutes apart, starting before he has to normally get up. Hide them in his bedroom – under the bed, in a wardrobe, behind some books. It would be really, really cruel to do this on a day he doesn't have to get up. But you probably thought of that already.

BRRNG!

Bubble Bed

Bubble wrap is fun to pop and even better to jump on. Put some music on and try to pop in time to the beat. You could put a piece under the doormat, so visitors get a surprise. But best of all is hiding a big bit under the sheet on the guest bed.

Mummy Race

PRANK!

Next time you're bored, get a fresh loo roll and ask a friend to wrap you up as a mummy. Do the arms and legs separately so you can lurch and grab at them. Then turn all the lights out, you hide in the dark and your friend has to find you. When they do, chase them while groaning . . .

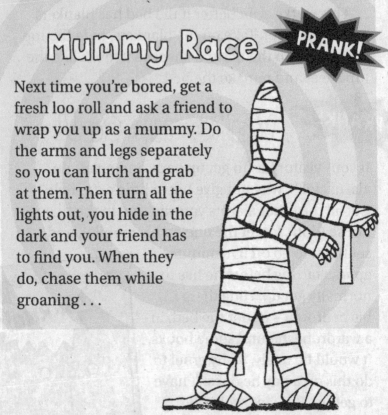

Sigurd Shadows

Only one of these shadows is the right one for Siggy. Can you work out which one?

Crusher of Worms Crossword

Dig up your knowledge on Sennapod to fill in this 4,600-year-old crossword.

Across

2 What pointy stone building is a mummy buried in?

3 Sennapod isn't a king, he's a _ _ _ _ _ _ _.

5 Which country is Sennapod from?

6 What are Sennapod's favourite animals?

Down

1 What are mummies wrapped in?

4 Sennapod is protected by the Curse of _ _ _ _ _ _.

Now you decide - which is better?

Pharaohs ☐   Vikings ☐

christmas vs Birthdays

Now this is really tough. If you had to choose, which would you rather have – Christmas or birthdays? Both have presents, obviously.

Birthdays usually involve parties and yummy food. The kids at Pirate School really know how to have a birthday bash (with actual bashing).

Christmas comes with time off school, but you have to see smelly relatives. And there's the remote chance of Father Christmas's evil brother using Christmas pudding to take over the world!

Father Christmas flung the rocket-sleigh into a handbrake turn and accelerated hard but it was useless. The *Death Pudding* had caught the little sleigh in its extra-sticky Sticky Matter traction beam and was relentlessly reeling in the rocket.

A gaping mouth appeared among the flames on the surface of the *Death Pudding* as the rocket was sucked inside. As the mouth began to close back down Father Christmas, peering fearfully from his sleigh, saw what he had most feared all his life – his big, bad brother!

Invasion of the Christmas Puddings

Why did Father Christmas get lost on Christmas Eve?
He was mis-sled.

Why was Father Christmas annoyed?
He left his sleigh in a Snow Parking Zone ... and got mistle-towed.

What did the Pringles say to the Skips?
'Happy Crispmas.'

What happens if you eat Christmas decorations?
You'll get tinsel-itis.

What kind of mobile phone has Father Christmas got?
Pay As You Ho, Ho, Ho.

What's the most popular wine at Christmas?
'Aww! Do I have to eat the sprouts?'

How does Good King Wenceslas like his pizzas?
Deep and crisp and even.

Why was the stable so crowded on Christmas Day? **Because of the Three Wide Men.**

I'm so excited – I'm going to have a puppy for Christmas!

Really? We're having turkey.

I got a pocket calculator for Christmas.

You don't seem too happy about it.

Well, I can already count my pockets.

What do angry mice send at Christmas? **Cross-mouse cards.**

They played 'Pin the Eyepatch on the Pirate' and 'Pass the Pistol', but the best game was 'Musical Cannons'. Everyone had to rush round the deck and when the music stopped they hid in a cannon. Ziggy fired one, accidentally on purpose, and Miss Fishgripp found herself far out at sea.

They had a disco too. Patagonia danced with Dick, who was very good at disco dancing. He even tossed Patagonia into the air, only to find himself holding her wooden leg, while Patagonia went flying up and up until she landed upside down in the crow's nest.

Pirate School: The Birthday Bash

What do you say to a cow on her birthday? **'Happy Birthday to Moo.'**

Where should you get a cat's present? **From a cat-alogue.**

Why shouldn't you give a cat a DVD player? **She'll only be able to press 'paws'.**

What's the worst thing to get for your birthday? **A pack of batteries marked 'toy not included'.**

I got given £5 for my birthday, but my cat ate it.

Never mind, at least you've got something in the kitty.

What's the best thing to put in a birthday cake? **Your teeth.**

What do cows play at birthday parties?
Moo-sical Chairs.

How would you feel if you forgot to give your goldfish a present?
Gill-ty.

How did Darth Vader know what Luke Skywalker was getting for his birthday?
He felt his presents.

What do you give a gorilla for his birthday?
I don't know, but you'd better hope he likes it.

Big Presents

PRANK!

You need a big pile of newspaper, a lot of tape and a friend. You'll also need some time alone in the room.

Wrap all the furniture in the room in newspaper – absolutely everything. Chairs, table, bed, wardrobe, TV (turn it off first). Leave the cat, though. And avoid precious things that might get broken. Use lots of tape.

Hide nearby to hear the moaning when your target comes back to find all their lovely 'presents'.

crunch cake

You may need an adult's help with this one. Turn a biggish cake tin upside down, make up some icing and . . . ice the tin. Lay it on nice and thick. Then decorate it with sweeties and candles.

To add a second joke, hide a teeny tiny iced fairy cake under the tin. When your victim discovers they can't cut their 'cake', say you're sorry and ask if they want their real cake.

Boo Balloon

Get two balloons, one light coloured (white or yellow) and one dark (red or blue). Write a message on the light one with a felt-tip pen.

Blow up the dark one nice and big, to stretch it, then let it down again. Stuff the light balloon inside the dark one, so the bit you blow up is still showing. Blow up the light balloon, and tie it off. Then blow up the dark balloon a bit more, and tie it off.

When you're ready, burst the dark balloon with a pin. It will appear to have changed colour with a bang.

Birthday Boogie

The Pirate School are strutting their stuff. How many stars can you find in this picture?

Christmas Pairs

These words can be joined together in pairs to make things with a Christmas connection. Can you match them up? The first one has been done for you.

STOCKING	WREATH
SAUSAGE	PAPER
WRAPPING	PIE
CHOCOLATE	FILLER
CAROL	CHAIN
MINCE	ROLL
PAPER	COIN
HOLLY	SINGER

Now you decide - which is better?

christmas ☐   Birthdays ☐

Mums VS Dads

This one's just too hard. Which is better: Mum or Dad? Maybe you've got a dad like Nicholas, who decides what his family really needs is a pet alligator. He also half-built a dinosaur-shaped giant slide in the back garden, but got bored.

Maybe your parents aren't quite that interesting. Tim Witkinson has the World's Most Boring Parents (and that's Official). Except when, to Tim's surprise, they're not.

Then there's my mum. She has an incredibly exciting job – she's a librarian! Sometimes when she comes in from work she's all a-flutter because something amazing has happened.

'You'll never guess what – Mrs Tuttle brought back her books and, do you know, there was a fly squashed inside one. She said, "I can't read this, it's got a dead fly inside." So she brought it back.'

Gosh.

Chicken School

Have you got any holes in your pants?

Of course not!

Well, how do you put them on then?

Mum, this soup tastes funny.

Well, why aren't you laughing?

'That's the one!' she cried. 'That's the bottom I'm after. Darling, you have the most gorgeous bottom!'

You should have seen Dad's face. He went red right to the tips of his hair and struggled for words. 'Th-th-thank you,' he said. 'Nobody's ever told me that before. Erm, yours is nice too.'

The woman stared back at Dad. 'What?' she said.

Dad stared at the young woman. 'What?' he answered.

My Brother's Famous Bottom

I think your bikini is rather small and revealing.

Well, take it off and wear your own trunks then.

My cousin is named after his father. **He's called 'Dad'.**

Why did it take so long for Dad to make chocolate-chip cookies? **He had to peel all the Smarties first.**

Dad walked in with a pig under his arm. **'Where did you get that?' asked Mum.** 'I won him in a raffle,' said the pig.

But we can't keep a pig at home! Think of the terrible smell!

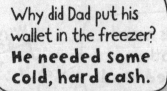

Oh, I'm sure he'll get used to it.

Why did Dad put his wallet in the freezer? **He needed some cold, hard cash.**

Suits You

If you go swimming as a family (with or without an alligator), a simple prank is to swap your dad's trunks with your mum's costume. Roll them up in their towels. Make sure they head into the changing rooms with the 'right' one.

Watch out, though – if Mum gets annoyed at having to get dressed again to come out and swap back with Dad, you may not get much of a swim.

How does Dad make anti-freeze?
He hides her woolly blanket.

Dad, why has your jacket got three arms?

It's from an arm-y surplus shop.

Mum and Dad go out twice a week to a lovely romantic restaurant for a delicious meal. There's candles and music and everything.

Sounds great.

Yeah, but Mum goes on Tuesday, and Dad goes on Thursday.

Dad, are caterpillars safe to eat?

Why do you ask?

There was one on your salad, but it's gone now.

Give them a break

Your parents might wind you up sometimes, but go easy on them. Remember all the things they have to put up with:

- Being treated as walking wallets
- Stepping on spiky toys with their bare feet in the middle of the night
- Having to memorize your lesson timetable and the names of all your classmates
- Clearing up after your birthday party
- Watching your *Fluffy Bunnies Go to Cuddletown* DVD for the fiftieth time
- Spending days tracking down that toy you want for your birthday – the one you don't really like by the time it arrives
- Explaining where babies come from
- Never getting to sleep late at the weekends
- Changing nappies. LOTS of nappies!

Crazy Couples

Untangle the lines to find out who goes with who. Then, for a really tricky challenge, can you name their children?

Now you decide - which is better?

Mum ☐ Dad ☐

The Strange History of the cosmic Pyjamas

Part Two

Ali (the alchemist, you remember?) was pretty gobsmacked by all this, as you may well imagine. He set out to discover what had happened and why. It had to be something to do with that stannidium stain. Ali tried staining a different piece of cloth. He touched it with a stick but nothing happened. He caught a mouse – there were a lot of them in the house – and put that on the stained cloth and still nothing happened.

Finally he took off his robe and carefully laid out the sleeve, stain uppermost. He dropped the mouse on the stain and –

KERRANNGG BAM BOOLLIE BANG!

The mouse vanished. Poor mouse. Who knows where it went? (Well, obviously the mouse knows, but the mouse isn't here, is it?) Ali smiled and nodded and hurried up to his bedroom. Why? Was he tired? No. It was because he wasn't wearing anything except his underpants. (He'd taken off his robe, remember?)

So Ali got changed and set about his next experiment. Slowly, bit by little bit, he realized that he could draw pictures with the wet stannidium. Once the ink dried the picture stayed on the cloth forever, but it had to be the cotton that came from Omar, the cotton that had been grown on the smashed-to-bits Stanley. (The comet, not the rabbit. *Do* pay attention.) Then, when the picture glowed or wriggled or sparkled, if you touched it that is where you would end up. And if you were lucky you might find a way back.

Even so, Ali had no idea how the magic lettering appeared, or how the mysterious pocket came about. They just happened. But Ali the alchemist did make the first pair of Cosmic Pyjamas. At least, they were not exactly what you'd call pyjamas – what he made was an all-in-one bodysuit, a bit like a jumpsuit with buttons down the front. (Otherwise you wouldn't be able to get into it.) The bodysuit was the first bit of clothing to have pictures all over it – pictures of pyramids and planets, stars and cars, palaces and forests, animals and mountains – anything that Ali could think of. There was even a rabbit somewhere. It might have been Stanley.

Ali himself tried out the bodysuit. He waited for something to glow – it was a forest. He touched it and that was where he ended up. So he picked a few bluebells, which of course you shouldn't do because they only die – very quickly. Anyhow, he picked some and waited for the picture of his home to wiggle and then he came whizzing back. And even though it all happened in the twinkling of an eye the bluebells had already wilted. See? I told you. DON'T PICK BLUEBELLS!

Not only did Ali have a handful of dead bluebells, he'd also got mud all over the bottom of his bodysuit, so he put it in the wash. Oh dear. That was a mistake. Do you know what happened? It shrank. It shrank to almost half its size.

Well, Ali was a bit upset about that as you can imagine. He wondered if there was any way of rescuing his work and after a while he got an idea. He cut the bodysuit in half, so now he had a top half and a bottom half, which, as you should have worked out for yourself, was a lot more like a proper pair of PJs.

Ali did the sewing himself. (He was quite good at ironing too.) He had to be very careful of course and make sure he didn't touch any of the pictures if they started to misbehave. So now Ali had a pair of cosmic pyjamas but they didn't fit him. They were only suitable for a child.

Now, next door there was a girl called Afet, and she was a bit of a nuisance. She was always pulling faces at Ali and sticking her tongue out at him. She thought Ali was a wicked wizard, especially when he went *kerranng bam boollie bang*. Well, you would think that, wouldn't you? Suppose you had someone next door going *kerrang bam boollie bang* all over the place. You'd be suspicious, wouldn't you?

Anyhow, Afet was a real nuisance. She didn't just pull faces. She made up rude songs about Ali and sang them in the street outside his house. Very loudly. So Ali put the cosmic pyjamas in some pretty paper and took them to the post office and posted them to her.

Two days later, Ali was sitting in his front room having a nice cup of tea when all of a sudden he heard a distant *kerrang bam boollie bang* from next door. Ali smiled, and guess what? He didn't hear any more rude songs and he never saw Afet again.

And neither did anyone else because Afet had been whisked off to Dinosaur Land. Of course this was a bit awkward, because Afet was wearing the cosmic pyjamas and now she was among dinosaurs. It took ages for Afet to find a way of getting out of there. In the meantime she was chased by a tyrannosaurus, nearly sat on by a brontosaurus who obviously had NO idea just how BIG his bottom was, and finally carried off by a pteranodon.

Luckily, at that point one of the pictures on the cosmic pyjamas wriggled. It was a picture of a bus. Afet touched it and suddenly found herself cruising round Trafalgar Square in the heart of London on a double-decker bus. The year was 2008.

By this time Afet had realized that the cosmic pyjamas were a bit tricky. So she went to the nearest charity shop and swapped them for some jeans with sparkly bits on them and a cool red

T-shirt. After a while she found a nice family to live with who thought the songs she made up were very funny. They were the Dean family and they had four cats and a hamster called Stanley. (Yes, I know it's a coincidence, but some people obviously like that name.)

You may be wondering how the pyjamas could have pictures of buses and stuff like that on them when Ali the alchemist lived at a time when buses hadn't been invented. And you may be wondering how Afet, who also came from long ago, knew about charity shops. In fact, you may be wondering about lots of things in this story. Well, all I have to say is that this is MY story and I'm telling it MY way and if you don't like it then you can go away and write your own.

In the meantime, if you like the idea of cosmic pyjamas that go *kerranng bam boollie bang* when you least expect it, and which have disappearing pockets and magic writing, then you will almost certainly enjoy reading the Cosmic Pyjamas stories. They are:

THE BATTLE FOR CHRISTMAS

KRANKENSTEIN'S CRAZY HOUSE OF HORROR

and Number Three - which doesn't have a title yet.

There are some amazing adventures ahead!

cops VS Robbers

This one should be easy: the cops are the good guys, and the robbers aren't. The trouble is sometimes it's hard to tell which is which.

Sergeant Smugg may be a policeman, but he's also a mean bully to Trevor and Streaker. They do manage to get their own back on him, with Tina's help.

Mr Tugg, the world's angriest man, is always on the lookout for baddies. He's in the Neighbourhood Watch, and is always trying to get people arrested when he thinks they're up to no good. Especially Nicholas's dad.

'Well, well, well,' sneered Sergeant Smugg. 'If it isn't our old friend Trevor Larkey.' He nodded at the security guard. 'I know this lad. He's always in trouble. Didn't have a dog with him, did he? Partners in crime, they are.'

The guard shook his head. 'Didn't see any dog.'

'Hmmm. Could be that while you had your eyes on this lad the dog was making off with a shopload of goods.'

Return of the Hundred-Mile-An-Hour Dog

Sarge, two prisoners have escaped: one is seven feet tall, the other's only four feet tall.

You'd better start searching high and low for them.

What did the peanut say when he came into the police station? **I've been a-salted!**

Why are police officers so strong?
Because they hold up traffic.

Why did the police arrest a cat?
Because they found all the cat litter.

A cannibal has just joined the police force.
He wants to grill the suspects.

Stop, this is a one-way street!

So? I'm only going one way.

But everyone else is going the other way!

Well, you're a policeman, make them turn round.

What did the policewoman say to her belly button?
You're under a-vest.

What do the police like on their toast?
Traffic jam.

Why did the book join the police?
So he could work under cover.

What did the duvet say to the sleeping policeman?
I've got you covered.

Why would Snow White be a good judge?
Because she was the fairest in the land.

I was about to rush upstairs to wake Dad when the burglar alarm went off. At least what actually happened was that the chickens went off. They were the alarm! They suddenly went berserk, led by their choirmaster, Captain Birdseye. You should have heard the shrieks!

A moment later Mr Tugg's searchlights fizzed on and the gardens were flooded with light. The burglar froze in panic, staring all around and then decided to make a run for it in our direction.

My Brother's Famous Bottom Goes Camping

Thieves have stolen two baths and a shower. **They made a clean getaway.**

The police are looking for a short psychic who's escaped from prison. **They say there's a small medium at large.**

The police are looking for a cowboy wearing a paper hat, paper shirt, paper trousers and paper shoes. **He's suspected of rustling.**

 Police have found a dead chicken. **They suspect fowl play.**

What do thieves eat at bedtime? **Milk and crookies.**

 Why did the baddy cut the legs off his bed? **He needed to lie low for a bit.**

Who steals soap? **A dirty rotten crook.**

Why did the burglar wear blue gloves?
He didn't want to be caught red-handed.

I've just had my watch stolen from right under my nose!

What a strange place to wear a watch.

When I grow up I'm going to follow in my dad's footsteps and be a policeman.

I didn't know your dad was a policeman.

He isn't, he's a burglar!

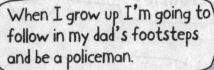

What do the police use to arrest bad pigs?
Ham-cuffs.

One Blind Mouse

Next time you're left alone with someone else's computer, take a look at the underneath of the mouse. It probably has a little red light in a hole in the middle. Take a little strip of tape and carefully stick it over the hole.

The mouse won't work until the tape is removed.

Spot the Tugg

Here's Mr Tugg in six unusual positions. Can you match each picture to its shadow on the opposite page? Draw lines to make pairs.

Fooled You

Warn your victim that April Fool's Day is coming up. Describe a few of the other pranks you've done (make up some horrible stuff, if you like). 'And what am I going to do this year?' you add. 'Wait and see . . .' And smile widely. Every time you see them, suppress a giggle.

When it gets to April Fool's Day, you won't have to do anything – they'll already have imagined pranks far worse than you could do.

Now you decide – which is better?

Cops [ ]   **Robbers** [ ]

Brothers vs Sisters

You probably know whether brothers are better than sisters. It's simple: if you're a girl, sisters are better. If you're a boy, then that's obviously wrong. Let's face it: brothers and sisters don't get on.

Carrie and Ben Lightspeed argue all the time, even when Sennapod orders them to stop. Max and Ellie fight constantly, until the Cosmic Pyjamas land them in the middle of a battle with an evil Christmas Fairy. And Jodie's brother Mark drives her mad, but she needs his help when she catches Dinosaur Pox. Maybe brothers (and sisters) aren't that bad after all.

Things Jodie doesn't like, number three: her brother, Mark.

She was ten and he was only nine, so how come he was already taller than she was? They got on like two scorpions shut in a box only big enough for one. (Not that it was ever Jodie's fault. She was the oldest, and full of common sense – how could it possibly be *her* fault?)

Dinosaur Pox

My brother's so thin that if he sticks his tongue out he looks like a zip.

I slept like a baby last night. **I woke up crying every two hours.**

My brother's so tall he has to stand on a chair to brush his teeth.

Why don't you take your brother to the zoo?

If they want him, they **can come and get him.**

A brother: someone who can reprogram a computer but can't make a bed.

Can Ben come out to play?

No, sorry.

Well, can his football come out to play then?

My brother lost three kilos in weight last night. **He had a bath.**

Sometimes there was no pleasing his sister. On the other hand he didn't want it to end like this. He turned round again. 'I wish you were back home, I mean, not as you are now, you know, as you were.'

'Mark, you didn't like me as I was. We were always quarrelling.'

'Yeah, I know, but . . .' He struggled for words. 'It was OK, wasn't it? I mean, we quarrelled, but everyone does that. I never wanted you to be a dinosaur.'

'Snap!' grunted Jodie.

'. . . and I wish you weren't. I just want you back home.'

Dinosaur Pox

My sister's so thin that when she sings she looks like a needle.

My big sister spends ages and ages in the bathroom. **She's a plumber.**

How do you keep an idiot in suspense for seven days?

I don't know, how?

I'll tell you next week.

My sister and I always have the same thing for breakfast. **Arguments.**

How do you know if a phone call is for your sister? **If the phone rings, it's for her.**

Pete says I'm ugly and Rob says I'm pretty. What do you think?

I think you're a bit of both. Pretty ugly.

Short Leg

PRANK!

You need to be able to sew for this one. Take a pair of your brother's school trousers and turn them inside out. Fold up the hem of one leg by two or three centimetres and sew it in place. If the trousers get washed and ironed before he puts them on, he'll never notice.

Point out to some of his friends in the playground that one of his legs seems to be growing longer than the other.

PRANK!

Arm Stretching

Complain to your little brother that you've been writing so hard that your arm's got longer. Could he help you even your arms out?

Hold your arms out in front of you, with your palms pressed together, and the fingers of your writing arm just a bit further forward. Ask your brother to pull on the other arm 'to even them up'.

When he's done that, hold your arms out again to check . . . only this time, the other arm is 'longer'. See how many times you can get him to stretch your arms before he catches on.

It's the kind of thing that can confuse a stupid person.

Who was that boy I saw you kissing last night?

Umm... what time last night?

When should you put a spider in your sister's bed? **When you can't find a frog.**

It's hard for my sister to eat. **She doesn't like to stop talking.**

My older sister got married in Mum's wedding dress.

How did she look?

Fantastic, but Mum was freezing.

My sister's so short that when she pulls up her socks she can't see where she's going.

Fizzy Fury

When your sister opens a can of fizzy pop outdoors, distract her attention by pointing out something off to the side. When she turns to look, quickly drop a strong mint in her can through the hole. Then move back swiftly – if it works, the drink will fizz up so hard it will squirt up out of the can. All over your sister! The reaction depends on the type of mint and drink, so try different ones to see what works best. And don't EVER try this indoors – it can get messy!

Laugh-your-socks-off Quiz

Test your knowledge of Jeremy's books with this fiendish quiz!

1 What is the name of the doctor who examines Jodie in *Dinosaur Pox*?

....

2 What are the twins Cheese and Tomato really called?

....

3 Name all of the Indoor Pirates.

....

4 Trevor's dog is Streaker, of course. What is the name of his friend Tina's dog?

....

5 In *The Beak Speaks*, what is the name of Mark's little sister?

....

6 Name the two professors who bought
Sennapod the Pharaoh back to life.

....

7 What are Nicholas's parents called?

....

8 How did Jack end up in hospital in *Beware!
Killer Tomatoes*?

....

9 Who is 'Mrs Green-Jelly' married to?

....

10 What is the name of Father
Christmas's evil twin brother?

....

Now you decide - which is better?
Brothers ☐   **sisters** ☐

Sorry, that's your lot! By now you should have made all your choices about which is better – hope it wasn't too tricky! You may want to check here again in a while, to see if you've changed your mind . . . or to remind yourself of some pranks and jokes.

Keep a note of your choices here:

Pirates	☐	**Teachers**	☐
Grannies	☐	**Babies**	☐
School	☐	**Hospital**	☐
Dogs	☐	**Birds**	☐
Aliens	☐	**Dinosaurs**	☐
Pharaohs	☐	**Vikings**	☐
Christmas	☐	**Birthdays**	☐
Mums	☐	**Dads**	☐
Cops	☐	**Robbers**	☐
Brothers	☐	**Sisters**	☐

Are you sure?

Oh yes, I agree!

NO NO NO!

You're wrong there

Absolutely.

That's not very nice

Ask Jeremy

Of all the books you have written, which one is your favourite?

I loved writing both **KRAZY KOW SAVES THE WORLD – WELL, ALMOST** and **STUFF**, my first book for teenagers. Both these made me laugh out loud while I was writing and I was pleased with the overall result in each case. I also love writing the stories about Nicholas and his daft family – **MY DAD, MY MUM, MY BROTHER** and so on.

If you couldn't be a writer what would you be?

Well, I'd be pretty fed up for a start, because writing was the one thing I knew I wanted to do from the age of nine onward. But if I DID have to do something else, I would love to be either an accomplished pianist or an artist of some sort. Music and art have played a big part in my whole life and I would love to be involved in them in some way.

What's the best thing about writing stories?

Oh dear – so many things to say here! Getting paid for making things up is pretty high on the list! It's also something you do on your own, inside your own head – nobody can interfere with that. The only boss you have is yourself. And you are creating something that nobody else has made before you. I also love making my readers laugh and want to read more and more.

**Did you ever have a nightmare teacher?
(And who was your best ever?)**

My nightmare at primary school was Mrs Chappell, long since dead. I knew her secret – she was not actually human. She was a Tyrannosaurus rex in disguise. She taught me for two years when I was in Y5 and Y6, and we didn't like each other at all. My best ever was when I was in Y3 and Y4. Her name was Miss Cox, and she was the one who first encouraged me to write stories. She was brilliant. Sadly, she is long dead too.

When you were a kid you used to play kiss-chase. Did you always do the chasing or did anyone ever chase you?!

I usually did the chasing, but when I got chased, I didn't bother to run very fast! Maybe I shouldn't admit to that! We didn't play kiss-chase at school – it was usually played during holidays. If we had tried playing it at school we would have been in serious trouble. Mind you, I seemed to spend most of my time in trouble of one sort or another, so maybe it wouldn't have mattered that much.

14½ Things You Didn't Know About

Jeremy Strong

* * * * * * * * * * * * * * * * * *

1. He loves eating liquorice.

2. He used to like diving. He once dived from the high board and his trunks came off!

3. He used to play electric violin in a rock band called **THE INEDIBLE CHEESE SANDWICH**.

4. He got a 100-metre swimming certificate when he couldn't even swim.

5. When he was five, he sat on a heater and burnt his bottom.

6. Jeremy used to look after a dog that kept eating his underpants. (No – NOT while he was wearing them!)

7. When he was five, he left a basin tap running with the plug in and flooded the bathroom.

8. He can make his ears waggle.

9. He has visited over a thousand schools.

10. He once scored minus ten in an exam! That's ten less than nothing!

11. His hair has gone grey, but his mind hasn't.

12. He'd like to have a pet tiger.

13. He'd like to learn the piano.

14. He has dreadful handwriting.

And a half . . . His favourite hobby is sleeping. He's very good at it.

Answers

Odd-Pirate-Out

1b has lost his elbow patch; 2c is missing an earring; 3a is in a good mood; 4c doesn't have a tattoo.

Toilet Trail

Trail D leads to the loo.

Spot the Difference

See right

School Search

D	N	U	O	R	G	Y	A	L	P
A	M	R	O	F	I	N	U	T	A
T	E	A	C	H	E	R	K	S	S
P	Y	C	L	N	G	R	S	L	O
S	L	O	C	K	O	E	E	U	B
S	E	R	E	W	M	E	D	N	P
A	S	T	E	B	T	R	B	C	U
L	S	M	L	O	E	U	R	H	P
C	O	Y	A	O	T	Y	S	H	I
H	N	B	O	K	L	A	T	E	L

Animal Antics
See right

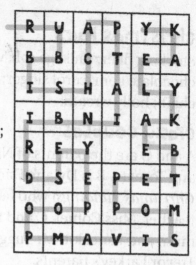

Alien Anagrams
EARTH; PLUTO; MARS;
VENUS; MERCURY;
NEPTUNE; SATURN.

Dinomaze
See below

Sigurd Shadows
C is the only
matching shadow.

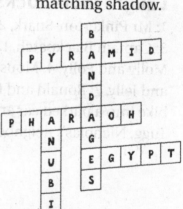

Crusher of
Worms Crossword
See right

Birthday Boogie
There are 27 stars in the picture
(don't miss the shoe buckles!).

christmas Pairs

Stocking filler; sausage roll; wrapping paper; chocolate coin; carol singer; mince pie; paper chain; holly wreath.

crazy couples

A and G are the parents of Nicholas, Cheese and Tomato. B is Dylan's Dad (*Invasion of the Christmas Puddings*) who fancies I – Dylan's teacher, Miss Comet. C and H are Nicholas's dad's mum and Lancelot, Mr Tugg's dad. E and F are Trevor Larkey's parents.

Spot the Tugg

A–3; B–5; C–4; D–6; E–1; F–2.

Laugh-Your-Socks-off Quiz

1: Mr Pinkerton-Snark. 2: James and Rebecca. 3: Captain Blackpatch, Lumpy Lawson, Bald Ben, Molly and Polly. 4: Mouse. 5: Tamsin. 6: Grimstone and Jelly. 7: Ronald and Brenda. 8: He rode his bike into a parked car and broke his leg. 9: Mr Tugg, Nicholas's neighbour. 10: Bad Christmas.